Tales From
The
Pod Auger Days

To order additional copies of this book, contact:
Xlibris
844-714-8691
www.Xlibris.com
Orders@Xlibris.com

ISBN: Softcover   978-1-6641-2443-1
         Hardcover   978-1-6641-2444-8
         EBook   978-1-6641-2471-4

Print information available on the last page

Rev. date: 09/04/2020

Tales From
The
Pod Auger Days

JEAN EDWARDS

Illustrated by: Jean Edwards & Laurence A. Edwards

Dedication

My introduction to the literary world was facilitated by my grandfather, George W. Fish. When I was a young child he would call me to the front yard of the farmhouse where we all loved to watch the rising mist as the sun rose. He would caution me to "Be quiet, and listen". Then he would tell me the name of each creature that would twitter or rustle as they awoke to start their day. When the sun was fully up my grandfather would go about his morning chores and I would engage in childish play. He had a vast knowledge of nature as he had studied their habits when he was a teenager by spending many nights burying himself in leaves and brush in order to study the habits of woodland creatures.

When George became an older teen he refused to attend school. The school superintendent visited the Fish family farm to investigate the problem of George's truancy. When questioned about his absenteeism, George replied, "Because I know more than the teacher. The school board can make up a test and if the teacher outscores me I will attend school". Said test was written and administered. George so outscored the teacher they fired him and gave George the job as school master. After teaching for years in various towns in the area he became the superintendent of schools and held the position for some time. Becoming tired of the politics of the position he bought a farm and decided to become a farmer, as there would be less argument from the animals, and he remained a farmer for the rest of his life. Education, however, was not forgotten.

His cherry roll-top desk that sat by the window in the large kitchen was filled with magazines and periodicals, all neatly stacked by category. I would make my way to the kitchen and he would look up and say, "What shall we read tonight?" We would each choose a magazine and sit at the table with our chosen reading material and quietly enjoy our literary pursuit and our companionship in the glow of the kerosene lamplight.

From George Fish came ten children and many grand and great grandchildren. Some became teachers, some nurses, shipyard iron workers, carpenters, sportsmen and women, musicians and military men. He never accepted a Social Security check, declaring that those government funds were there to help those unable to work and support themselves. One of George's ten children was Roger Fish, who is the main character in this book.

George never really gave up teaching and I was a most ardent student. Farmer, yes, but teacher, most definitely. What a wonderful world it would be if there were more teachers like George W. Fish. Therefore I dedicate this volume in his memory.

Jean E. Edwards

Contents

Great Grandpa Builds His House

When Great Grandpa was a little boy he went to school in a one room schoolhouse on Appleton Ridge. The ridge was really almost a mountain overlooking the town of Appleton, also known as McLain's Mills, nestled along the St. George River. The schoolhouse was quite large. Great Grandpa always called the bygones the "Pod Auger" days. That was his special name for them. His father was the schoolmaster and he was very strict. The children wrote their lessons on small slates which they kept in their desks, and they studied geography out of big green geography books. It was hard being a schoolboy when his father was the teacher, but Great Grandpa worked very hard to make good grades which pleased his father. He had many fond memories of happy days with his friends at the school on the ridge.

When Great Grandpa grew up and became a man raising a family he decided to build a house. He wanted to build his house down in the village of Appleton. He bought some land near the center of town on which was a stone cellar. The house had burned down years before. It was called "the Arnold place." Great Grandpa built a tiny little cabin on the land hear the cellar to live in while he planned and built his house. First he started working on the cellar, straightening the walls and replacing the rocks that had fallen down. While he was working on the cellar he remembered the old abandoned schoolhouse of his childhood that was still standing on the ridge. The beams were thick and sturdy and it was built carefully to last a long time, the way they did in the "Pod Auger" days. He decided to buy the schoolhouse where he went to school as a boy and make it into his new home.

The town was willing to sell him the old schoolhouse so Great Grandpa made his plans. First, he measured the cellar at the Arnold place, then he went up on the ridge and measured the old schoolhouse. The schoolhouse was much too large, but the beams were thick and wide, so he got an idea. He would cut the schoolhouse in half because half of it would fit the cellar exactly!

It took a long time to cut it in half because there was no electricity in the old schoolhouse, so he could not use an electric saw. He had to use a big hand saw and carefully saw back and forth, back and forth with his strong arms, until he had cut the house in half. He took some boards and a hammer and nails and carefully braced the house so the walls would be strong, because the next problem was to move the house from Appleton Ridge down to the village in the valley below. Great Grandpa could not afford to hire big machinery to move his house down to the village. He knew he would have to figure out how to do it himself. Great Grandpa decided the only way he could move it was to cut some trees, trim off the branches to make round logs and place the logs under the house like big wheels or rollers. He would tie ropes to the schoolhouse and with a team of horses he would pull it along, and when the house moved forward far enough the last log in back would be left behind, and he would stop pulling, run back and get the free log and drag it to the front and put it under the house. Then he would drag the house forward again until the next log in back was free and he would bring that log to the front, and so on. It would be slow work, but that did not discourage Great Grandpa, so he sat at the kitchen table and had a bowl of Addie's bread pudding with a glass of goat's milk and planned his route. There were two roads to the valley. The road to the right was the shortest distance, but alas, it was also very steep. That might be a problem. How would Great Grandpa stop the house if it started rolling too fast? He decided to go to the left; it was farther but the road down to the valley was not as steep. It would take days of hard work, and Great Grandpa was just a little man, but he was determined! The next morning after a breakfast of eggs and biscuits he rolled up his shirt sleeves and began to move the old schoolhouse.

Soon the old building was at the crossroads of Pitman's Corner. Great Grandpa had a problem. The power lines crossed there and the house was too tall to go under them. The road was very narrow and the power lines were too low. What would he do now? He couldn't go ahead and he couldn't go back, for it would be uphill going back, and the house would be too heavy for the horses to pull. Great Grandpa was discouraged, but not for long. He got another idea! He would call the power company! Yes! They would come and help! They came and moved the power lines so Great Grandpa could roll the old schoolhouse through Pitman's Corner.

What a sight when the house was finally coming down the main street of the town! Everyone cheered! Great Grandpa did it! He built his house out of the old schoolhouse and put it on the Arnold place, and his family would be snug and warm and safe from the winter cold. They were very proud of Great Grandpa and of the house, and the house made from the schoolhouse that traveled from the top of Appleton Ridge to the Georges River Valley below still stands in Appleton Village today.

Great Grandpa Digs His Well

Great Grandpa built his own house to live in because he liked to do everything himself. He was a carpenter by trade, but he was always reading and studying so that he would know how to do all kinds of things. He liked to invent new contraptions and make things with his own hands. He didn't want to buy things in a store if he could figure out a way to make them himself. Mostly, he liked to build houses, but one day when he was carrying water from the spring across the river, he got an idea. He decided to dig his own well.

The first decision Great Grandpa had to make was where to dig his well. He knew some men decided where to dig a well by using a forked branch from an apple or cherry tree. It was called a "divining" or "dowsing" rod. They would hold the branch by the two ends with the larger branch out in front "just so" and walk across a field, and when the stick pointed down toward the ground they would declare it was the place to dig a well. Great Grandpa found a branch from a cherry tree and he walked back and forth, back and forth across the pasture, waiting for the stick to point to the ground so he would know where to dig his well. The divining rod never did point to the ground. Maybe his arms were too strong. He was sure there was water under the ground in his pasture because all his neighbors on that side of the road had wells in the pastures behind their houses. He knew water ran in veins deep in the rock under the pasture, so he looked to the left and he looked to the right and he decided to put his well in line with all the neighbors' wells. He was sure he would find water. "This is where I will dig my well," he said, and he started digging.

First great Grandpa used a shoved to dig. He made a small round hole in the earth. There were lots of rocks. It was very hard to dig, even though his arms were very strong. He went to his barn and got his mattock. His mattock was a tool with a three foot handle. There was a heavy metal attachment on the end that had a square shaped blade on one side and a pick on the other. He lifted it high over his head and swung it down to the earth. It made a great thudding sound as it struck the rocky soil. Over and over Great Grandpa swung the heavy mattock. He used his shovel to scoop up the loosened dirt and broken rocks until the well was deep enough to stand in. Day after day he dug until he could no longer shovel the dirt out of the hole. He was deep in the ground in his well hole. Up from his well he climbed and built a frame over the well and tied a bucket to it with a long rope. He climbed back down and lowered the bucket down in his well and filled the bucket with the loosened dirt. Using his rope he pulled the bucket of earth to the top where a school boy emptied it on the ever growing pile of dirt beside the well.

One late afternoon, just as the sun was going down and he was getting ready to quit for the day, Great Grandpa's feet felt strange. It was dark down in the well and he couldn't see much and he wondered what was wrong with his feet. Suddenly, he knew!! His feet were getting wet!! Faster and faster he dug, sending more dirt up from the well -- and soon there was an inch of water in the bottom of the well where he stood. He climbed up his ladder, jumped out of his well, and ran across the pasture in leaps and bounds, shouting to his family, "Water! Water! We've got water!" How happy everyone was, and Great Grandpa was busy figuring, "One inch of water in five minutes means 1 gallon in five minute, six gallons in half an hour, twelve gallons in an hour," and so on. He was very excited when he ran back to his well the next day, expecting his well to be filled to the brim, but alas, there was still only one inch of water in his well. He had found only a small pocket of water, not the vein of water he needed. So he started digging again.

Several days passed and one day when he struck the earth to loosen it, "clunk," came the sound. Again he tried to loosen the dirt. Clunk," the sound came again. Great Grandpa had struck solid rock. Up he climbed from the well hole. Down from the pasture he stomped. "Addie," he said to his wife, "I have to blast. I know there is water down there, and I'm going to get it!"

The next weekend Great Grandpa had what he needed: dynamite, caps, fuse wire and a battery to "detonate," or explode the dynamite. He used a small chisel and day after day the townspeople could hear him up in his pasture, down in his well, "clink, clink, clink, -- clink, clink, clink," was the sound as he made holes in the solid rock to secure the dynamite. Addie was very nervous the day Great Grandpa was ready to blast his well. His children were nervous. The neighbors were nervous. This was the most dangerous thing Great Grandpa had ever done, and everyone was very worried.

There was a great quiet in the village. Then, "Boom!!" There was no mistaking the sound. Great Grandpa had blasted his well. He came bounding down across the pasture, safe and sound, but what a sight he was! Black soot covered him from head to toe and only the whites of his eyes were visible! A very happy Great Grandpa was safe and the well was filling with water. Maybe it had a slight taste of gunpowder for weeks, but Great Grandpa had dug his well.

Great Grandpa Builds His Garage

Great Grandpa loved his house he built from the old ridge school, and he decided he needed a garage to go with it. He didn't have much money but he had some leftover lumber from building his house and he had an idea. There was a steep bank beside his house on the far side of the driveway. That was where he would build his garage. He wouldn't need a lot of lumber and he wouldn't need a bulldozer to flatten the bank – because he would build his garage IN the bank. Great Grandpa got out his chalk line, his blue chalk and his measuring tape. He found two sticks and pounded one in the ground where he wanted his garage to start, measured sixteen feet and pounded the other stick in the ground, then tied his chalk line to the sticks. He took his blue chalk and rubbed the string all the way from one stick to the other, pulled up on the middle of the string and "TWANG." When he let go the chalk line snapped against the dark earth leaving a straight blue line on the ground, showing exactly where his garage would be. He did the same thing to mark where the sides of his garage would sit against the bank, and then he was ready to dig. He got his mattock down from the barn. He got his shovel down from the barn, and he got his wheelbarrow down from the barn. Then he began to dig. It was too much to finish in one day, so Great Grandpa worked a little every day. First he would use the mattock, "thunk, thunk, thunk," and the sod and dirt would loosen up. He saved the top layer of grassy sod and put it to one side; he used his shovel and put the dirt in the wheel barrow, then he pushed the wheel barrow up to the pasture and emptied it in a soggy place that needed to be filled.

Several weeks went by and soon Great Grandpa had a big hole in the bank. He found some heavy beams among his lumber and made a stout frame in the hole that would be his garage. He built sides to his garage and then he put beams across the top and nailed on a flat roof. He gathered up the grass sod he had saved and put it carefully over the boards and made a nice sod roof. Then he filled in some holes around the sides. He was proud of his new garage. It was like the sod houses they built in the Old West – but something was missing. He needed a door to his garage. He measured the front of his garage and he measured his lumber. He had just enough! He built a good, sturdy door. It was very heavy so he put strong hinges across the top to fasten it in place. He needed a way to pull the heavy door down into place so he went in his house to think. "Addie," he said to his wife as he drank a cup of coffee, "I think I've figured it out!" Great Grandpa had a plan. He would use a pulley to close the door, with a heavy weight to pull it down tight! Up to the barn he hustled where he found an old clam hod that was like a wooden box with a handle. He filled it with old bolts and car parts until it was heavy enough to pull the door shut. He set up his pulley and tied the heavy bucket of bolts and metal to the pulley attached to the door – and Oh-Oh, - the door slammed shut with Great Grandpa inside!! No one knew Great Grandpa was trapped inside his garage. The door was very heavy. The dirt walls of the garage were very thick. No one heard him calling for help. It was getting dark. Addie wondered why her husband stayed out working so long when it was supper time. Finally she went out to the garage and called, "Roger! It's supper time!" and she heard his faint answer, "I'm in here. Pull on the door, Addie!" Addie pulled on the door and the door opened with the help of the bucket of bolts. A jubilant Great Grandpa jumped out and exclaimed, "It works, Addie, just like I knew it would!"

Great Grandpa's Mercedes

Many people in the little village of Appleton had shiny new cars. Great Grandpa watched them drive up the main highway with the sunlight dancing on their hoods as they approached the village. Sometimes he wished he had a shiny new car but he didn't have enough money to buy one.

One evening he sat down in his favorite chair, the one he had built himself from an old wooden bed. It was solid oak and had a cushioned seat. He sat in his chair and warmed his feet against the side of the black iron cookstove as he read the newspaper. He glanced at the "FOR SALE" section, and his sharp blue eyes stopped where it said, "Foreign Auto for sale, cheap."

Folding his newspaper under his arm, he hustled down to the general store to use the telephone. He and Addie had never had a telephone in their house, as he figured if a person didn't have anything really important to call about, no phone was needed, and if something important did come up he could use the one at the general store. The car was still available, so he made an appointment to see it. A friend took him there and he bought the little red Mercedes. The reason it was being sold at such a low price was because the motor was burned out, so they had to tow it home.

Great Grandpa was very proud of the little sports car. He knew he could make it run again. It needed a new motor so he went to a junk yard and looked through all the old wrecked cars until he found a poor smashed Mercedes that had a good motor. The only problem was that it was a diesel motor and the sports car he had was supposed to run on gasoline. That did not discourage Great Grandpa. He would make it work somehow, so he bought the diesel motor from the junk man.

Many days went by with Great Grandpa working away on his Mercedes in his garage beside the house. Often he came in the house greasy and tired, but undaunted. Wires had to be changed, hoses had to be changed, motor mounts had to be changed. Finally he had the new motor in place, and a satisfied Great Grandpa closed the hood of his sports car – almost. The new engine was too tall, the hood would not close down.

Searching into the wooden tool box where he kept his oiled and polished tools he took out his hack saw. Carefully he cut a square hole in the hood of the car and softly he closed the hood. The hood clicked shut. Rubbing his hand over his whiskery chin he eyed the sports car thoughtfully. The way it was, he couldn't drive it in the rain because the engine would get wet and might stall, or even rust. Besides, someone might make fun of a sports car with a

square hole in the hood, and he was too proud of the little car to let that happen. Then he remembered. He had seen pictures in auto racing magazines of race cars that had an extra piece of metal on the hood called a "scoop." He would find one and it would cover the hole and look sporty too!

The auto supply store had just what he needed and soon he had it riveted in place. There was just one problem, it was gray and did not match the rest of the car. Back he went to the auto store and came home with a paint brush and a bucket of paint.

What a surprise it was when Addie looked out and saw the little car was a blazing orange, hood scoop and all!

With his best felt beret set on his head at a rakish angle and Addie by his side, there was no prouder man in town than Great Grandpa in his own shiny sports car!

(The Mercedes has been restored to its original condition by his grandson Larry Edwards.)

Porky Runs Away

Great Grandpa loved animals. He had a cow, a sheep, a burro, some goats and Porky, his dog. Porky was a black and white Boston terrier. He had a stubby little body and a little pug face. His ears were soft and floppy but they stood up stiffly when he became excited. Great Grandpa taught Porky many tricks. Sometimes Great Grandpa would have Porky put on a show. Porky loved to show off and would race through the house and run fast and jump through a hoop or over a broomstick. Great Grandpa always held the stick low so Porky wouldn't miss and feel disappointed. Sometimes Great Grandpa would fix an evening snack and Porky always wanted some. He would look longingly at the food until Great Grandpa would say, "If you want some, Porky, you'll have to lick your lips." Then Porky would put his tongue out a little bit more. But Grandpa would say, "Now Porky, if you want some, you'll have to do better than that. You'll have to REALLY, lick your lips!" Then Porky would run his tongue out as far as he could and lick his lips all around. Great Grandpa would laugh and give Porky his snack.

One Day Great Grandpa let Porky out in the yard for a little play time. After a few minutes he called, "Porky! Time to come in." No Porky came. Great Grandpa went out and looked all around, calling "Porky! Porky!" He went up to the barn. He looked in the pasture. He called, "Porky!

Here, Porky." No Porky came. Great Grandpa was angry with Porky. He always came when he called before. Where could he be? He walked up the hill by the house calling, "Porky! Here, Porky!" He went down the hill by the river. "Porky! Here, Porky!" But no Porky came. He went up by the Baptist church. He went to the general store, but no one had seen Porky. Great Grandpa was very sad. Two weeks went by and Great Grandpa missed him very much. There was only one thing to do. He would get another dog. He heard about some pups for sale so he went and bought a furry little black spaniel pup. He named the puppy "Bozo," and he decided he would teach Bozo all the little tricks that Porky used to do, and then he wouldn't miss Porky so much.

He was sitting in the kitchen with the new puppy when he heard a knock at the door. It was a neighbor who said, "Roger, I think I saw your dog on the road to the ridge." Great Grandpa jumped in his car and drove up the hill to the ridge. About a mile up the road he saw a shivering black and white dog in the gutter by the side of the road. Yes, it was a skinny, hungry, thirsty Porky with very sad eyes huddled in the gutter. Great Grandpa stopped his car and tenderly lifted the little dog in his arms - "Well, Porky," he chuckled, "When you get home you will see you have a new playmate, and when you realize someone came to take your place, I guess you won't run away again." And he never did.

Bozo Gets A Haircut

When Porky ran away and Great Grandpa got another dog, it was a very different kind of dog. Porky was a short haired Boston terrier so he never needed a haircut, but the new dog, "Bozo," had thick curly black hair that was growing longer every day.

The weather was getting hotter as spring turned into summer. Great Grandpa looked at his two dogs. Porky, the short haired dog, seemed to be really happy frisking about the yard, but Bozo looked too hot. Porky would run and play and chase sticks and butterflies, but poor Bozo would just lie around and pant.

Great Grandpa decided Bozo needed a haircut. He thought if Bozo had a haircut he would be cool and would run and play like Porky. Great Grandpa had a nice pair of sheep shears. After all, he had shorn his sheep this spring and the sheep was running happily about the pasture, chewing the buttercups and grasses and enjoying the warm weather. He decided a good haircut would be just the thing to make Bozo a happy dog. Bozo was a good dog and sat quietly while Great Grandpa clipped his hair. He trimmed his ears a little first so Bozo would "get used to the shears." Next, he cut the hair down his back shorter than his belly because the hair wasn't as long there. Off went he fluff from Bozos tail. Finally he got to Bozo's legs. He cut the hair short down to the ankles on all four legs – and then he stopped. "There, Bozo," he said, "You'll be cool now, and you can run and play with Porky, but I've left you some fuzzy slippers to keep your feet warm."

Some people thought Bozo's haircut was strange indeed, but Bozo was proud of his haircut and his fuzzy slippers, and ran happily off to play.

Great Grandpa Cuts the Brown Bread

Great Grandpa liked to do things the way they did in the olden days, and he liked the old traditions. He always looked forward to Saturday night, because it was a custom in New England to have baked beans on Saturday night. He liked the sweet brown crusty piece of pork that was snuggled down in the syrupy beans, and best of all was when his wife, Addie, made fresh steamed brown bread to go with them.

Addie always mixed up a whole-wheat batter made dark with molasses. She poured the mixture in empty coffee cans and set them in a large kettle half filled with boiling water where they steamed until suppertime. The kitchen was warmed by the black iron wood stove, the baking beans and the steaming kettle sending vapors throughout the room until the air was filled with fragrant promise of the coming evening meal.

When Great Grandpa came in with firewood gathered from the snowy forest, the supper would be ready. Sometimes it would be very cold outside and the windows would be etched with frost from the steam in the kitchen, making icy gardens and cornfield patterns on the glass. The children would come and sit around the table and wait solemnly while he washed up for supper. When Great Grandpa was ready at last, the steaming bowl of beans was placed in the center of the table and Addie carefully lifted the coffee cans of brown bread out of the bubbling kettle. She held the cans carefully with potholders and ran a knife around the inside edge of the cans, separating the cooked bread from the edges, until slowly, slowly out came the round rolls of brown bread onto the waiting platter.

The yellow country butter was ready to spread, and the children were ready and anxious to eat, but they waited quietly for Great Grandpa to slice the bread. He would say, "Addie, the string," and Addie would hand him the piece of white string that she had saved. It was the same piece of string that had come tightly wound and tied around the white paper package of salt pork from the general store. It was the piece of salt pork that had cooked all day in the stoneware bean pot and now crowned the bowl of beans before them.

Great Grandpa gently laid a roll of bread on its side and wrapped the string around it about a half inch from the end of the loaf, then carefully he crossed the string ends and pulled. Slowly the string cut through the hot bread and it tipped off the roll, steaming deliciously as it fell.

The first slice he handed to Addie, wrapped the string evenly around the end again and a second piece was sliced from the roll, then a third and fourth until all were fed – and each slice was perfectly formed, and none were sticky as they would have been if they had been cut with a knife.

There was no finer meal on a New England Saturday night than when Great Grandpa and his family followed tradition.

Great Grandpa Has A Visitor

One day Great Grandpa was sitting at the kitchen table in the little house he had built, drinking a cup of rich dark coffee he had perked on the black iron woodstove. He was thinking about his children and grandchildren and how he missed them since they had all moved away. As he was looking out the window wishing someone would come for a visit, a car drove up and stopped in front of his house. It had "out-of-state" license plates, but he recognized his granddaughter so he jumped up and ran out to greet her. A fellow he had never seen before was with her and after they were introduced Great Grandpa invited them in. He was overjoyed as he and his wife Addie always had doughnuts and cookies on hand and the coffee pot on the stove in hopes of company. After they had a snack, Great Grandpa said to the young man, "Come up to the pasture, I want you to see my animals." They went up through the rustic, bark covered gate to the pasture on the hill. This was where the brown and white Toggenberg goats pranced in the warm sunlight, and the soft white sheep grazed on the tender shoots of grass.

Great Grandpa kept his animals clean and brushed and well fed, as they were his little pets, but his pride was in Pedro, the burro. He had trained the burro to sing for his supper. He would offer him some grain and say, "You have to sing if you want your supper." Pedro would give a little nod to his head and just blow a little air out his mouth. Great Grandpa would say, "Now Pedro, that is not singing, if you want your supper you have to really sing." Pedro would shake his head and blow a little harder and make a little whistling sound. Great Grandpa would say, "Now Pedro, you have to REALLY sing if you want your supper," and finally Pedro would say, "HEE-HAW," and Great Grandpa would give him his supper. Great Grandpa showed his visitor how he had trained Pedro so he could walk up to him and suddenly grab his nose or pull his tail and Pedro would stand calmly and not move an inch. He told him he did that every day so if a child came up and touched Pedro he would stay calm and not kick.

Pedro had always been a good and gentle burro. He showed how his burro would give his dog Porky a ride on his back. When Pedro walked in a small circle and gave just a short ride to Porky, he said, "I mean a REAL ride, Pedro," until Pedro took the little dog for a ride all around the edge of the pasture.

Suddenly Great Grandpa had another idea. He would show the city boy how he could ride on the back of his burro. Addie came out to watch. She folded her arms across her chest and shook her head. She did not think this was a good idea but she knew Great Grandpa was determined, and he was. He took the reins in his hands just so – and climbed up on Pedro's back. He sat proudly on his burro when suddenly Pedro lowered his ears and "BUMP!". He suddenly bucked and jumped and Great Grandpa went flying. His glasses flew one way – his false teeth came out and flew the other way, and Great Grandpa landed on his seat on the ground. Great Grandpa was very angry. Pedro had ruined all the fun by being stubborn and bad. Great Grandpa picked up his glasses and put them back on his head. He found his false teeth and put them back in, and he found a small switch growing nearby. He was hopping mad. He said "You miserable jackass!! I'll teach you to throw me on the ground!" Great Grandpa was never cruel and only tickled Pedro's backsides with the little switch, but he scolded and shamed him all the way to the barn, where he had to stay for the rest of the day. Pedro had to really sing for his supper that night but he had learned his lesson – and Robin Baker, the young man from Boston, had a day to remember.

Great Grandpa Names the Baby

Great Grandpa had four daughters, Virginia with the golden curls, Joyce, the tomboy, Jean, the serious one and Brenda, the youngest. He taught all his children to work hard. When the wood had to be stacked beside the house for winter he showed them how to make the stacks even so they would be neat and make the job of fetching wood for the winter fire easier. The sticks were laid "just so" to prevent the stack from falling when one or two sticks were removed. The garden was always a source of pride to Great Grandpa and he taught the girls to pull the weeds carefully so the plants would grow green and strong. He taught them how to milk the cow, and often one of them would hold the planks of wood steady when he was building, or bring him tools as he needed them.

Great Grandpa sometimes thought it would be nice to have a boy in the family, but he thought it over and decided his family was great just as it was. He would sometimes brag that his girls could do more work than any of the village boys, and do it better. One day Addie said she had an announcement. What a shock it was when she told him that a baby was on the way! After all, they were not young anymore and Great Grandpa had thought his family was complete. He thought many nights about it and decided he would name the new baby Benjamin, after his uncle, Benjamin Keller, who was a doctor in a nearby town. He could hardly wait for spring to arrive as the baby was to be there for Easter.

On April sixth the new baby came. Addie was very quiet, for she worried that Great Grandpa might be disappointed, but a happy Great Grandpa bounded into the room and looked at the little dark haired bundle. "She's beautiful", he exclaimed, "and a fifth girl will always be welcome!"

And that became the new baby's name, "WELCOME."

Great Grandpa Gets His Christmas Goose

Christmas was always a special time of year for Great Grandpa. He always went about his work singing, "Christmas is coming, the geese are getting fat. Please put a penny in the old man's hat." After teaching the rhyme to his small grandchildren he would give them one of his old hats to carry around, and if they would say the rhyme he would give them a penny. Of course back then, a penny would buy a nice piece of candy at the general store. He was especially fond of the little Christmas rhyme but even more fond of the tradition of having a goose for Christmas dinner. He always said turkey was fine at Thanksgiving and chicken at other times of the year, but he just had to have a goose for the Christmas feast.

One cold and snowy December Great Grandpa was very glad he had planned ahead for his Christmas goose. It was one of those New England winters when snow came early and the air so crisp and frosty the snow did not melt between storms, and many of the country folk were snowbound on their farms for days at a time. Great Grandpa was very pleased with himself for having ordered his goose early from a man who was raising geese about six miles from the village. It gave him great pleasure thinking about his goose getting fatter and fatter every day on the goose farm. He didn't want to get his goose early, he wanted his goose to be as fat as possible for the Christmas feast. He was glad he didn't have to get a goose from the freezer at the grocery store. He wanted a fresh goose for Christmas, so he decided to go after his goose on December twenty-fourth.

Way in the night on December twenty-third it started to snow. The snowflakes were small and soft at first. Then the flakes grew a little larger. They tumbled down faster and faster and began sticking together in clusters. Under the streetlamps in the village square they looked like small snowballs falling to the ground. Silently the snow came, and softly if piled higher and higher on the quiet fields, on the dark evergreens and on the quiet streets, as the town slept through the winter night.

By morning the snow was very deep. No cars could travel. The snow plows were busy on the big main highways. The little town was "snowed in."

Great Grandpa jumped out of bed. He started the fire in the black iron kitchen stove to warm the kitchen and start a pot of coffee. Then he looked out the window. The snow was almost up to the window sill and all the streets were quiet. He was very discouraged. How was he to get his Christmas goose if he couldn't get his car out to go after it? Suddenly he got an idea. He slapped his sides and chuckled out loud! He had a friend who had a snowmobile! He would borrow the snowmobile and go after his goose!

Great Grandpa's friend was glad to lend him the snowmobile but warned him it might give him trouble as it had not proved itself completely reliable. Great Grandpa was sure he could handle any problems so he bundled up in warm clothes for the trip. He put on long underwear and two pairs of warm trousers, one pair over the other. He put on his warm wool mackinaw with the furry lining over his flannel shirt and pulled a heavy woolen cap down over his ears. Carefully he folded a newspaper and put it across his chest under his jacket so the wind could not chill his body. He put tough leather mittens over knitted woolen gloves and on his feet, leather boots over several layers of socks. He had made his boots waterproof by melting suet in a pan on the stove and dabbing the liquid grease on his boots until every surface and seam was waterproofed. Lastly, Addie tied a scarf to cover his face so that only his bright blue eyes could be seen.

Addie had her doubts about her husband's great goose adventure, but she helped all she could, as always. She knew it was still snowing and the wind was starting to blow. She feared blizzards, and the snow was getting deeper by the minute, but there was no stopping Great Grandpa from getting his Christmas goose. He started up the snowmobile and off he went, with a roar of the motor and a wave of his hand – like Santa wishing "to all a good night", Addie thought.

Time seemed to drag as Addie busied herself in the kitchen. She made mince pies and an apple pie and a cake for Christmas dinner and a bread pudding full of plump raisins for Christmas breakfast.

Supper time came and no Great Grandpa had returned. It began to get dark. The snow was very deep, and it was getting very cold. What if the snowmobile had turned over? What if her husband was somewhere in the snow, being covered with thick snowflakes?

Finally, at 8 o'clock Addie heard a shuffling sound, and a noise at the door. There stood Great Grandpa, looking like a big snowman, a very cold Great Grandpa with a very cold and stiff goose in a cloth sack. "It was tough, Addie," he said, "the snowmobile broke down and I had to walk, but here it is! I've got my Christmas Goose!"

Great Grandpa Goes Hunting

In the Pod Auger Days the men went hunting every November, hoping to bring home meat for the winter. Times were poor and they needed the meat to go with the home grown vegetables and for the mincemeat pies at Thanksgiving. Great Grandpa had harvested a big garden. He had weeded and hoed until his garden had been a thing of beauty. He always worked very hard to make his vegetable worthy of a prize at the county fair.

One year when November rolled around Great Grandpa decided he would go hunting. He had been thinking about a great stew with carrots and potatoes and venison, and it made his mouth water. He had bought an old shot gun at an auction and he polished the brass fittings and oiled the wood until it shined like a museum piece. It hung on the wall in the kitchen where he could look at it and think about eating his stew.

The day the hunting season opened Great Grandpa remembered something he had to do, so he couldn't go that day. The next day he thought of something else he had to do, and Addie could see him up in the barn puttering around. Every day he remembered something he had to do, and finally it was the last day of hunting season so Great Grandpa put on his red plaid mackinaw and hat, took down his weapon and announced that he was off to the woods. Addie worried all day about Great Grandpa being in the woods. She didn't like this hunting idea but she always supported her husband in all of his adventures. She wished he would hurry up and come home so she could stop worrying. She cooked supper and made an apple pie and some biscuits and hoped he would be there to eat them. Dusk came and suddenly an excited Great Grandpa burst through the door. "Oh, Addie" he exclaimed, "You should have seen it. It was a beautiful deer! He held his head high and proud with his beautiful antlers shining in the evening sun. He leaped in the air and ran across the field with his white tail bobbing as he ran. What a beautiful sight! Too bad I missed!"

Everyone knew by his description of the scene that Great Grandpa was to gentle to shoot a deer, but they went along with the story. After all, he did hunt for a deer, and Great Grandpa, the hunter, had found one.

Great Grandpa Builds a Camp

Building things was Great Grandpa's favorite pastime. He liked to do things the way they did in the olden days, or the "Pod Auger Days," as he called them. He made knives from old broken saw blades and made the handles from deer horn. If someone found deer antlers in the woods they would bring them to him for his knife handles. He made leather cases for the knives so they wouldn't be dangerous. He even wore one on his belt because he thought it looked sporty, and besides, it came in handy when he needed to whittle a piece of wood or cut a piece of string.

He made leather vests from thick tanned leather and sewed pockets on the front. Sometimes he sewed his vests with fine wire so the seams would be strong. He even sewed the seams twice, because he always did things the very best he could. When the second world war came there was a great shortage of shoes and everyone was allowed only two pair a year and his children wore out shoes very fast, so he decided to "build" shoes for his children. He sat up late in the evenings drawing a pattern on a brown paper bag, until finally he said, "Addie, I've got it figured out. I'm ready to build." Sure enough, he made fine leather sandals for his girls to wear during the summer months, saving their shoe allowance for winter shoes.

One day Great Grandpa became upset because the cost of getting his carpentering saws sharpened was too high. He built a frame to hold his saws steady and he would file the teeth of his saws until they were so sharp they would cut through a piece of wood almost as fast as the electric saws they use today. He loved his evenings warming himself by the black iron cook stove and planning things to build and do, but the country was at war, and Great Grandpa wanted to help.

It became necessary to move to a town on the coast because Great Grandpa got a job there in a shipyard. He worked on small wooden ships called "minesweepers." They were called that because it was the job of that particular ship to hunt for mines that might be floating in the water overseas. Nails and screws could not be used on the hull, wooden pegs had to cover any metal that was used to hold it together. Great Grandpa was an adzman, he used an ax-like tool to carve the boards on the ship's hull. He even invented a special device to make the adz work better, but to his disappointment someone else had already invented it. The long days working at the shipyard often grew tiresome so great Grandpa and the other workmen found ways to make the workdays lighter.

They didn't have water balloons then so they would fill a paper bag with water, run up the ladder to the scaffolding on the ship, race around to the other side and try to get there in time to drop it on a worker below before the bag soaked through and burst. It became quite a game and Great Grandpa would come home chuckling and guffawing over who got wet that day, but sometimes it would be Great Grandpa who came home soaked to the skin. One day he came home with a long wooly tail pinned to the back of his britches and Addie knew someone had thought of a new game, a "pin the tail" trick.

Even though he had a good job and good friends to joke with, Great Grandpa missed his home in the country. He wished he were back in the little town of Appleton where he could hear the river running at night and he could build things on his little homestead, but he felt he was helping his country and saving lives by working on the minesweepers. One day he got an idea. Since they lived in an apartment near the shipyard he got permission from his landlord to build a little cabin in the back yard. He was happy to be building again, and he planned to keep his tools in the cabin and it would be his own place, sort of a den. He thought about his cabin every day at work and every night after supper he would work on his camp. It was small but he managed to put a small couch and a hot plate in it so he could make a pot of coffee and relax and think up more things he wanted to build.

One day one of his daughters came home from school and said she didn't feel well. Great Grandpa and Addie exchanged glances. There was an epidemic of scarlet fever going around. They called the doctor and he said to Great Grandpa, "If you plan to go to work the next three weeks you had better leave right this minute. I am putting this house under quarantine."

Great Grandpa knew he had to go to work every day to earn money so his wife and children would be fed and clothed, and a quarantine meant no one could leave the house or go in the house for three weeks. Antibiotics had not yet been discovered and the streptococcus germ was very dangerous in those days. People thought the germs traveled onto anyone near a person with scarlet fever. Great Grandpa was worried. Who would see that Addie and the girls had everything they needed? What if they ran out of groceries or coal for the stove? Suddenly the answer came to him! He would live out in the cabin in the back yard! Every day Addie could put a note on the door and he would leave whatever the family needed on the steps! How lucky he was to have gotten the idea to build a cabin, it would save the day!

His daughter recovered, no one else in the family became ill, and they never forgot how Great Grandpa took care of them through the epidemic of '44.

The Dance Contest

Great Grandpa loved to dance. Regular dances were held at Riverside Hall on Saturday night. Great Grandpa was happy when Saturday night came around so he could take his wife, Addie. Sometimes there would be a Country Western Group and they would put on a show before the dance. The performers would sing all the popular "cowboy" songs of that time, such as "You Are My Sunshine," "I Want To Be A Cowboy's Sweetheart" and "She Taught Me To Yodel." Many of the singers could yodel very well, usually ending their yodel by holding the last note as long as they could until everyone applauded. They had comedy acts and lasso twirling and the crowd favorite, "the whip." A bull whip would be brought out and the performer would snap and crack the whip, then demonstrate how he could hit a small target with the end of the whip from across the hall. It was very scary for those in the front row but they trusted the cowboys. Sometimes they would even snap a cigarette from the mouth of a brave volunteer from the audience.

After the show the settees would be moved back against the wall and the dance would begin. There was a piano player, a fiddle player, perhaps a banjo and several guitar players. They played all kinds of songs but when the fiddle player started playing a square dance tune they all knew it was time to dance "The Lady of the Lake." The couples came forward for the contra dance and lined up, the ladies on one side of the hall and the gents on the other. Every other one would "cross over" to the other side until the lines formed on each side alternated ladies and gentlemen. When the music began they faced the person next to them and start "swinging" which was close dancing in which the couple would whirl around and around in one place until the "caller," (usually the fiddle player), would call out, "down the center." The couples from one side would "break" (stop swinging), and the gent would take the lady by the hand and lead her down the center of the hall and then take her to her partner to swing. It was amazing how it all worked out, and there were two contra dances each Saturday night. At intermission hot dogs were served. Great Grandpa always bought Addie hot dogs. He said she liked them better than anyone he ever knew, and sometimes he would buy her one at the end of the evening to eat on the way home.

Great Grandpa danced all the dances, but he liked waltzes best. He liked the faster "hop waltz" when the music was happy and he bounced his steps to show a little "hop" in the step, and the hesitation waltz, when the music stopped on the beat for a half second and the dancers were to hesitate mid-step, then resume the waltz. But Great Grandpa's favorite was the "Old Fashioned Waltz." He loved to glide around the room with Addie, who always followed his lead perfectly, and he would spin on his toes as he turned. One night they had a waltz contest and they put chalk on the bottom of the heels of the men's shoes before the contest started. When they chose the winners they checked the shoes, and any man who had put his heels down and had worn off the chalk was disqualified. The old fashioned waltz was supposed to be danced on tip toe, and the heels were never supposed to touch the floor. Great Grandpa was quite debonair with his polished shoes, his bowtie, and his neatly pressed tweed jacket, and as they whirled around the room Addie thought he was the best looking man there. When the winners were announced it was Addie and Great Grandpa who won the prize. Not a bit

of the chalk was worn off the bottom of the heels of his shoes! It was quite an evening but it was not over. A fight broke out at the end of the hall and several men engaged in fist cuffs. Addie became frightened. She became so frightened she fainted. Great Grandpa lifted her in his arms and started for the door but the fighters blocked the way. He held Addie in one arm and made a fist with the other hand and thrust his arm straight out at the fighters. They quickly dodged Great Grandpa's fist and his fist went through the wall near the door. He carried Addie down the stairs to the car and soon Addie was all right and they drove home. They had enough excitement for one night, but the hole in the wall stayed there for many years, even until his children were old enough to point it out to their friends, when they told about the night Great Grandpa won the dance contest and saved Addie from harm.

The Legacy

There came a day when Great Grandpa went away. He had lived a long and happy life with his wife Addie, and he raised five daughters in a loving way. He had worked very hard and one day his heart just gave out.

Everyone in the village was very sad. They would miss seeing him ride through the town on the special cart he had made, pulled by his burro, Pedro. His jaunty, cheerful air and the way he wore his special hats and caps to one side to accommodate his carpenter's pencil behind the opposite ear was a part of the daily sights in the town.

Great Grandpa's family felt a deep loss, but they knew he would not want them to be sad. They found good homes for his animals because there were too many for Addie to care for, especially when the weather got colder and the snow came. His family wanted to do something special so they could feel close to Great Grandpa even though he was no longer with them. They decided to go clamming because it was something Great Grandpa loved to do.

In cars and vans they all drove to Blue Hill, where the tide came in over a flat shore and made a place called "the clam flats." It was not a sandy beach. It was a black mud beach. This was a place to dig clams.

The air was misty and cool so they put on hats and jackets and boots. Armed with clam hods and clam forks they trouped down through the flats. It was harder than they thought. The mud was sticky and clung to their boots. Sometimes they sank in and got stuck, especially the grandchildren. They all hunted for the little bubbles rising up to the surface of the mud, because that was the tell-tale sign that a clam was down below. Carefully they pushed the clam forks into the soft mud; carefully they turned the mud over and picked the clams out and placed them in the wooden hods. They were very careful not to break any clam, because Great Grandpa had tried to teach them to dig with care so no clam would be damaged. It took many hours to dig enough clams to make a meal, but at last the hods were full and the tide was slowly coming in, covering the flats with frothy sea water. They let the water wash over the clam hods to wash away the mud, then they made their way back up to the edge of the beach.

A fire was built in a pile of rocks and seaweed gathered and placed on top, then layers of clams and more seaweed. The smoke from the fire and the steam from the cooking clam-filled seaweed mingled with the ocean air. They sat quietly until the clams opened their shells to announce that they were ready and the group ate their fill, put out the fire and cleaned the beach until it was as if no one had been there. As they left the beach to start home, they knew that somewhere, somehow, Great Grandpa was smiling.

Printed in the United States
By Bookmasters